Consultant, Istar Schwager, holds a Ph.D. in educational psychology
and a master's degree in early childhood education.
She has been an advisor, consultant, and content designer for numerous parenting,
child development, and early learning programs including the *Sesame Street*
television show and magazines.
She has been a consultant for several Fortune 500 companies
and has regularly published articles for parents
on a range of topics.

Louis Weber, C.E.O.
Publications International, Ltd.
7373 North Cicero Avenue
Lincolnwood, Illinois 60646

Manufactured in the U.S.A.

8 7 6 5 4 3 2 1

ISBN 1-56173-481-0

active minds

shapes

PHOTOGRAPHY
George Siede and Donna Preis

CONSULTANT
Istar Schwager, Ph.D.

Publications
International,
Ltd.

circle

A wheel, a donut,
buttons, a ball,

Bubbles to blow,
    the clock on the wall.

square

MY BOOK

A checkerboard,

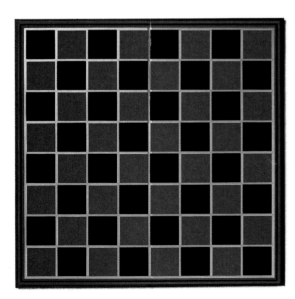

blocks, a
picture book,

A birthday present—
open and look!

rectangle

Building bricks, a window,
a wooden front door,

Crackers, and a puzzle
to work on the floor.

triangle

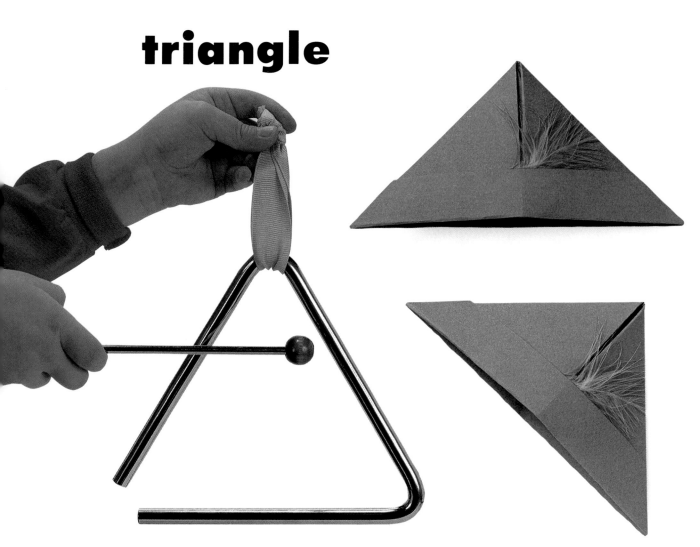

A musical toy,
   two hats made for fun,

Two flags flying high,
a tent just for one.

heart

A locket, some candy,
a Valentine cake,

A fancy I-love-you
card you can make.

oval

Eggs and grapes,
a balloon on a string,

Pussy willows
you find in the spring.

star

Stickers and badges,
starfish from the sea,

An ornament topping a Christmas tree.

diamond

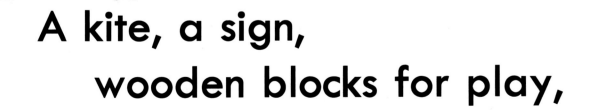

A kite, a sign,
    wooden blocks for play,

A cookie cutter,
and shapes cut from clay.